CAUTION!

This book is not about typos or putting misplaced commas in their rightful place. That's what retired schoolteachers who write letters to the company president are for. (And, yes, schoolteacher is one word.)

I'm here to help you identify, correct and avoid the minefields and misguided thinking that happen when you go about the business of attracting more business. They're lessons I learned on the frontlines of marketing, as founder and CEO of my own business. It was a national ad agency and marketing firm that helped all kinds and sizes of clients market their products and services and grow their business.

I don't have an MBA. So, if you're looking for theory and rhetoric, put the book down now, or ask me for a refund. If you're looking for tangible tools and creative ideas you can use right away to stand out and get better results from your marketing, keep reading.

~Terri Langhans~

The 7 Marketing Mistakes Every Business Makes

(And How to Fix Them.)

by

TERRI LANGHANS

The 7 Marketing Mistakes
Every Business Makes (And How to Fix Them)
Copyright © 2003 Terri Langhans

ISBN: 1-59196-278-1

First Printing June 2003
Second Printing February 2004
Third Printing January 2005
Fourth Printing April 2010
Printed in the United States of America

For information:
Speaking: www.BlahBlahBlah.us
Marketing: www.MaverickMarketing.com
Blog: www.AnythingButBlah.com

To Mom:

For dreaming that
someday you would walk into a bookstore
and see your daughter's book on the shelf.

And for giving me the dream
of making yours come true.

Thank you:

John, Patrick, Timothy, Kelsey,
Mark, Donna, Dean, Runk, Ron,
Marlowe, Greg, Starbucks,
Harry and Jesus.

Mistake #1

Marketing is something we "do."

Before I started my own firm, I sat on the client side of the desk as Marketing Director and/or PR Person for several different companies. No matter what industry I was in, regardless of how big or small the budget was, there always seemed to be a line of people out my door, and they all wanted the same thing. They all said the same thing:

"We need to do some marketing."

Many times it came out, "*Quick*, we need to *do* some marketing." The italics in their voices meant that the end-of-the-month numbers were coming up short, they weren't getting prospects to return phone calls, or the competition had just "done" some marketing and someone upstairs demanded to know "why aren't *we* doing stuff like this?"

"Do" some marketing. To this day I flinch when I hear it. Because when you say you're going to "do" some marketing, you've just pigeonholed the entire marketing process into running an ad, sending an email, doing a blog post, printing a brochure, writing a press release, throwing a special event.

Marketing communications—that's what you're talking about, and they are, indeed, part of the marketing mix. But just one part. The promotion part. And when you think of marketing only as promotion and communication activities, you're not making the most of what marketing can do to bring you more business. Marketing is much more than mere communication.

Marketing is a process, not promotion.

The marketing process is not deciding whether to run an ad or mail a postcard or do both and more. It's not about coming up with a clever headline or wrestling with an art director over how big to make your logo.

I say the marketing process boils down to these three questions:

1. Where are you?

2. Where do you want to go?

3. How are you going to get there?

You might say, "We sell 10 widgets a month, and we want to sell 20." Or "I bill $10,000 a month in consulting, and I want to bill $15,000." "I sell two houses a month and want to sell three." You get the idea.

Once you know where you are and where you want to go, ask yourself that obvious third question: How am I going to get there? Specifically, what am I going to do to get there?

"I know! I'll *do* some marketing! I'll do some *more* marketing. Direct mail, print advertising, a flyer, a blog and some articles. That'll do it," you say.

Can you hear how ridiculous that sounds? How narrow and limiting it is to think that just "doing" some promotional activities will get you all the way from where you are to where you want to go? It's going to take a lot more than promotion.

The Fix: Expand your definition of marketing.

Marketing is not just sales, advertising, promotion or public relations. All of those activities usually show up on the organization chart with lines connecting them to the box labeled "marketing." But if those are the only things you think of when you think about marketing your business and attracting more of it, you're missing out. Your marketing will be more effective if you expand your definition of it.

Don't panic. I'm not going to drag out the American Marketing Association's mouthful of a definition. Here's one I like better:

Marketing is anything that helps or hinders the sale or use of your product or service.

Anything. Anything that helps or hinders the sale or use of your product or service. If your retail business has a great storefront, the coolest stuff inside and competitive prices, but there's not enough parking, it's a marketing problem. Lack of parking hinders the sale of your product, and doing more marketing ala promotional activities will not help you increase sales. In fact, it could actually hurt your business.

If I have to make a U-turn to enter your parking lot, wait in line at the register, search too long for your address on the web site, deal with a less-than-informed employee, talk to a machine too often, call you before I can send a fax, or fill in way too many fields on the order form, it's a marketing problem. Those things might cause me to change my mind, call someone else or just give up and continue doing what I was doing or using what I was using.

If I hire you to provide a service, and your billing is complicated, you don't do what you say you'll do, when you say you'll do it, or if I hire you and the only person I see is a junior staff person, it's a marketing problem. Those factors hinder my use of your services, and I probably won't buy them again.

And none of these issues have anything to do with promotion. They have to do with your product or service itself—price, customer service, location, employee attitudes, administration and training. They have everything to do with marketing, because they can either help or hinder someone's decision to buy your product. They have everything to do with whether you're going to get your business from where it is now to where you want it to be.

A tool you can use.

Here's how you can turn this expanded definition of marketing into a tool that will make your marketing more effective. First look at where you are and where you want to go with whatever product or service you're going to market. Quantify it and put a fuse on it. (As in, how much and by when.)

Next, brainstorm a list of everything that helps the sale or use of that product or service, and make a list of everything that hinders or gets in the way of the sale or use of that product or service.

Once you have that list together, get out of the brainstorming mode and, as my Uncle Morris used to say, put on your thinking cap. Look at what's getting in the way and decide what and whether you can do anything about removing those obstacles.

Some things on your list will be out of your control. Like the economy, war and pestilence. Get over it. Some things, like the concrete median that forces people to make a U-turn at the intersection instead of hanging a left directly into your parking lot may seem to be out of your control, but you can look for ways to adapt or compensate.

You can't re-zone or re-route the traffic, but you can make sure that the map you print on your materials calls attention to the obligatory U-turn, and you can mention it in written or verbal directions, too. That way the customer isn't surprised or frustrated. You've made it easier for them to buy from you.

When it comes to the things that are helping you attract customers and win business, you don't need me to tell you to keep doing them. (But I will.) Do them better, regularly or perhaps more often.

As you look at the results of the Help or Hinder Exercise, your marketing strategy will begin to take shape. Go back to the connect-the-dots, get-from-here-to-there marketing process model. You know where you are and where you want to go. You have a list of what's helping and hindering your progress.

Come up with no more than a handful (that would be five) things you need to do, areas you need to address, to get where you're going.

Take me, for example. I might look at my list and decide that if I'm going to get my Maverick Marketing Workshop where I want it to be, then I need to do four things. (In marketing lingo, these would be called strategies.)

1. Increase visibility and awareness of the workshop.

2. Explore joint venture opportunities with people or companies that already offer workshops and seminars.

3. Get an online shopping cart and merchant account so that I can make registration simple and spontaneous.

4. Book six speaking engagements with marketing and business associations so that members who might be potential participants can "sample" my ideas.

Here's what your strategies might sound like:

1. Increase visibility and awareness for yourself, your product, service or business. (Maybe all four.)

2. Change the perception that you're a small fry consultant between "real" jobs.

3. Develop relationships with referral sources who can bring you lots of clients, instead of trying to get the clients one by one. (An advertising copywriter, for instance, would market to ad agencies and design firms who already have a roster of clients, versus trying to market to individual clients directly. For a lawyer, it might be a strategy to target CPAs or financial planners with clients who need trusts and wills. For me, it would be marketing to a speaker's bureau.)

4. Secure a line of credit.

5. Hire an operations person to free you up to be the rainmaker.

Did you notice something about my example and the hypothetical one? Did you notice that only one strategy in each example had anything to do with marketing communications?

It was "Increase awareness and visibility." That's the one and only strategy that will involve "doing" some marketing ala the promotional activities mentioned earlier.

But the other strategies, like getting a credit line, hiring more staff and accepting credit cards are critically important business development activities that will take you from where you are to where you want to be.

Now what?

Don't pigeonhole marketing into mere promotion. If you hear yourself thinking you need to "do" some marketing, expand your definition of the word and look all around your business, before you do anything or spend a dime on getting the word out.

Mistake #2

We believe in magic.

Just run an ad. Do that trade show. Speak to the Chamber of Commerce, mail that brochure, send another email, write a newsletter or get that press release printed. And *POOF*, people will come, call or throw money your way. Right away.

I wish the real world worked that way. But it doesn't. Yet we still operate as if it does, hanging on to unrealistic expectations of what marketing, and especially marketing communications, can do.

I attended a networking luncheon where the meeting-goers moseyed from table to table between courses to discuss various marketing topics. I chose a table hosted by a graphic artist who was sharing design tips.

She asked the assembled throng if we wanted to know a secret that would increase response 20 percent from our printed materials or ads.

Are you ready? (That's what she asked us two times before revealing the secret.) Here it is:

Put your phone number in italics.

I almost stabbed her with my salad fork. Let me get this right. All I have to do is put my phone number in italics, and I'll get 20 percent more business? Yep. Because you see, she said, italics convey urgency and action. It's magic.

No it's not. It's hogwash.

Advertising, and other marketing communications tools (with or without italics) don't sell anything to anyone. That's not their job. Their job is to make people curious. Give them enough information and inspiration to inquire. Get them to raise a symbolic hand and ask a question, go to the web site, reply to the email, pick up the phone, drive by the store, agree to a conversation.

Your marketing communications can bring the proverbial horse to water, perhaps even make him thirsty. But what if the trough is crowded, or the water tastes funny? Don't shoot the wrangler. He did his job.

The Fix: Get real.

Advertising and marketing communications can do three things. Selling isn't one of them.

1.   They can increase awareness and visibility.

They get the word out and can keep it out, for as long as you have your wallet out. They can get you on a prospect's radar screen and help you stay there. If one of your obstacles in Chapter 1 was "nobody knows I exist," or "my company might as well be invisible," then yes, absolutely. Marketing communications, and perhaps paid advertising, are right for the job.

2. They can create an image or personality for your company.

Just as you close a letter with your personal signature, your advertising and marketing communications can reflect and establish an image that is uniquely yours, as well. Especially if you're in a business where everyone looks alike. In fact, your marketing communications may be the one and only thing that sets your product or service apart from the competition by virtue of the voice or personality it reflects.

3. They can generate response.

Hold the phone! Didn't I just go on and on about how marketing communications and ads don't sell anything? That's OK, because I haven't contradicted myself. They can and do generate response—in the form of phone calls, foot traffic, requests for information, web site visits and so on.

Sure, once in a while, depending on your business, you might luck out with an unexpected order from someone in immediate need who saw your flyer. But don't bet your budget on it.

Your ad, flyer, email or other communication vehicle is not enough to close the "sale/no sale" decision in most cases. Create curiosity. Generate a conversation. Prompt a question. That's what they can do.

Then what about measuring ROI?

If marketing communications don't necessarily sell, then how do you know if they're working? How do you justify your marketing dollars or respond to some of these all-time favorites from the Bean Counter Hit Parade?

"If we give you more money in the budget, how many more widgets will we sell?"

"If the marketing doesn't work, do we get our money back?"

"The marketing didn't work. Sales are the same this month."

"The marketing didn't work. We would have gotten that business anyway."

They all reflect unrealistic expectations, punctuated by a few fingers pointed at the marketing department or marketing person, which very well might be you.

By now you know that marketing is not a department. It's everyone's job to deliver on the promises made in the marketing communications. But how do you spread that gospel and still be held accountable for realistic results?

Define the terms for success up front.

Before a word is written, a strategy is agreed to, or a dollar is allocated, you've got to get the Powers That Be and the powers that have purse strings involved in the process. From the beginning. Right from the "where are we?" and "where do we want to go?" stage.

If you're going to measure the results of your marketing, and you want to be held accountable for realistic performance, then you have to make sure the key players understand the situation (where are we?), agree to the goal (where are we going?) and pinkie swear that they think the strategies being discussed have a high likelihood of getting you there. And make sure that "doing some marketing" is not the only strategy they're counting on to get you there.

Once you've got everyone headed in the same direction, here are the two things you measure:

1. The ultimate goal or destination, as in widgets, clients, projects, sales, bookings and such.

2. The key indicators of success along the way, as in outbound and inbound phone calls, web site hits, and other response benchmarks that would indicate you're on your way to the ultimate goal.

Don't wait until the end of the sales cycle or fiscal year to measure progress. Measure those key indicators of success daily, weekly and monthly.

For me, if I want 20 people in my Maverick Marketing Workshop each month, I would measure response to the following marketing communication activities:

• Five outbound calls to prospects per week

•100 workshop brochures distributed at networking meetings.

• Email blast with the upcoming workshop as the lead story sent to 4,000 newsletter subscribers.

Key indicators of success, then, would be the number of emails and phone calls from people who want to know more about the workshop, the number of conversations that those inquiries generated, and then the ultimate number of people who register.

If whatever you do and measure is not producing the results you want, it's time for a mid-course correction. And remember, the mid-course correction may not have anything to do with the advertising or the marketing communication. The communications could be doing their job, but there might be a problem down at the trough.

Or the call center. Like when the bank's president told me the campaign "wasn't working." Yet when I looked at call center volume, it was up. The phone was ringing more than ever, so where was the roadblock to success? I started by calling the call center.

"I read something about a program you have for school kids, something where the bank sends a speaker to teach kids about savings and checking accounts? Can you tell me how that works?"

"Oh, that was just a publicity thing we did to get some press in the local paper," she said.

Egad. The campaign was working fine, thank you very much. And it was a good thing I was on the phone, unarmed, nowhere near a salad fork.

Now what?

Get real. If there is any magic to marketing, it's in the mix. Let the communications do their job, and then make sure you (and everyone else) does theirs.

Mistake #3

We breathe too much of our own exhaust.

Who knows more about your product or service than you do?

It's not a trick question.

"No one" is the right answer.

Of course you are the expert, and you should be, when it comes to what makes your product or service the right choice. Attributes and benefits roll right off your tongue. Technical specs and details are tattooed on your brain. Your mission statement is poetic, and you can practically dance to your tag line.

The competition? Ha! I better not get you started, right? You've got a boatload of reasons and a cost-to-benefit ratio spreadsheet locked and loaded, ready to blow them out of the water.

You are such a big believer in your business that you can't wait to show it off. You inhale the excellence of those features and benefits, and you exhale it with every breath, right into your marketing communications.

The problem is, when you do that, your marketing is all about you. And Dale Carnegie was right when he said that people don't care about you. "They care about themselves," he said.

So if your marketing is all about you, and people don't care about you because they care about themselves, then, by virtue of what I can remember about the reflexive property extolled in my high school geometry class, people don't care about you or your marketing.

But wait! There's more.

Not only do people not care about your marketing, they avoid it. They've built an elaborate defense system, like a wall of protection around their hearts, minds and lives to keep unwanted marketing and sales messages away from them.

You do the same thing. Think about it. Step away from your business world, take off your marketing hat, and think like a normal person for a minute.

On any normal given day, do you wake up in the morning all excited, full of anticipation, and say to yourself, "Gosh, I sure hope someone markets something to me today! I sure hope I get to hear a sales pitch or two"?

"No" is the right answer. The normal answer.

We all have our defense systems, our walls of protection. In my home, at the Langhans household, I conducted in-service training with my family. They know that if someone on the phone asks for Mrs. Loffhands, Lighthouse or Lederhosen, the right answer is "Sorry, wrong number."

Mispronouncing my name sets off my radar. Alert! Here comes a marketing message or a sales pitch. We all have that radar. And when a normal person's radar goes off, what do you do? Duck and cover behind the wall. Send it to voice mail. Hit the delete key. Throw it in the trash. Turn the page. Zap the commercial. Move to the networking table that doesn't have vendor lurking over it.

That's normal consumer behavior. You do it. I do it. All God's children do it. But then you go to work and put your marketing hat back on. Instant brain damage!

You forget what it's like to be normal. You do what most business people do when they go about marketing their business. They go at that wall with everything they've got. They whoop and holler, jump up and down outside that wall. Brag about their benefits, pound their chest and pound on the wall, trying to get someone to "open up" and pay attention.

The sad thing is, regardless of who's outside the wall, to the person on the inside, everyone sounds the same: "Hey, over here! Look at me! Ain't this great? Wanna buy some?" Blah, blah, blah.

Everyone is selling something. They're all talking about themselves, instead of the customer. They're certainly not talking about something the customer might care about.

The Fix: Connect before you convince.

Before you can convince someone you're the right choice, you have to connect to something they care about. Which we know isn't you. It's them. Your marketing has to be customer-focused, not all-about-you focused. It has to connect, before it can convince.

Here's an example. AT&T sells cellular phone service and cell phones. They could market that service and product by doing a TV commercial that shows the product, shows how it's affordable, portable and allegedly gets good reception all over kingdom come. That's the convincing approach.

AT&T didn't show that in one of my all-time favorite commercials. They showed a working mom packing lunches, getting ready for work with her two little girls skipping around her in the kitchen. One of the little girls asks sweetly, "Mom, don't go to work today. Take us to the beach. Puhleeeeeeeeze!"

"Sorry, sweetie. I can't take you to the beach today. I have an important client meeting."

After a sad moment of reflection and then reluctant acceptance, the little girl asks, "Mommy, when I grow up, can I be an important client?"

Gulp. Choke. I wanted to hug my daughter. Except that I was on a business trip. AT&T had my attention.

In the next scene, by the way, Mom and her girls are at the beach. Mom is talking on her cell phone, and the little girls are skipping around her beach chair singing, "we're having a meeting, we're having a meeting."

No comparison charts or product descriptions. AT&T brought the benefit to life, and more importantly, they connected it to something I cared about. They connected to me. They showed that they understand my world and how to make it better. They didn't get "over my wall." I peeked over, unlocked the door and invited them in.

You don't have to advertise on TV to connect. Here's a tool you can use to be customer focused, instead of breathing so much of your own exhaust.

What's important?

Step 1: Describe your product or service. Have at it. Get it out of your system.

For AT&T, it might sound like this: Nationwide cellular service with 1000 anytime minutes for $79 per month, phone included free for a limited time.

Step 2: What are the attributes or "attraction factors" that your specific target audience will like about your product or service? Not everything, just a select few that would spark their interest or set you apart from the competition.

For AT&T that might be that the phone is small, portable and gets good reception just about anywhere.

Step 3: What are the benefits of those attributes? And it's important to note that when I use the word "benefit," I am referring to the need or the want that is satisfied by your answer to Step 2.

In the AT&T saga, imagine the working mom saying, "Well, gee, if I had a small, portable phone with good reception, I could get my work done anywhere."

For the purpose of the exercise, state the benefit in first-person singular, as if your prospect is saying it. It keeps you focused on the customer's point of view, not your own tendency to tout your wares.

Now go deeper. Go beyond the benefit and look for meaning. Why is that benefit important or meaningful to the target audience?

Step 4: Look at the benefit you identified in Step 3 and ask yourself, "Why is [the benefit] important, personally, to the target audience?"

For AT&T, why is "being able to get her work done anywhere" important, personally, to a working mom?

"Well, if I could get my work done anywhere, I'd have better work/life balance."

Keep asking the question, replacing the benefit statement with the recent answer: Why is "work/life balance" important, personally, to a working mom?

"If I had more balance between work and home, I wouldn't have to miss any Mommy Moments."

Bingo. That's where AT&T chose to connect, to create a story and bring the benefit to life. They showed that they understood the world of working moms first--before they tried to convince. That's what got me to peek over the wall and pay attention.

Now what?

When you use the four steps to find your connection points, keep asking the "why is that important, personally" question over and over. You'll end up with a list of wants and needs, words and phrases you can use in your marketing communications and sales conversations. Words that attract, not repel.

It's not about you. Focus everything on the customer and what they want. Don't try and get through, over, under or past their wall. Connect before you convince, and they might just invite you inside for a chat.

Mistake #4

We ask the wrong questions and accept the wrong answers.

People have two reasons for everything they do. The real reason, and one that sounds good. I'm paraphrasing J.P. Morgan. He may not have been a marketing maven, but he was right about human nature.

Go ask your neighbors why they bought that expensive car. Which answer are you going to get? The one that sounds good, most likely. J.D. Power ratings, *Consumer Report* safety statistics, resale value, performance. Yeah, right.

We all know the real reason, don't we? But we also know the neighbor's not going to admit it.

The same thing can happen when you do marketing research. You've got to be careful. You've got to make sure you're getting the real answers, the ones that will give you insight, not just information that sounds good.

Now I'm going to paraphrase a story I heard Guy Kawasaki, former Apple marketing exec, tell about Sony boom boxes. Remember when they first came out, those portable CD/AM/FM stereos? They were about the size of a small microwave oven with a handle? Remember how, after a while, they came in bright blue, yellow, orange or hot pink plastic?

That's because Sony did research with young people, and when Sony asked the young people what color the boom boxes should be, they said, "not black." Black was the color their parents would buy, and no way would a cool kid want to carry around a boring black boom box.

The day-glow colored boom boxes didn't sell too well, though. So Sony did some focus groups and asked what color the boom boxes should be. "Not black" was still the answer.

But this time, when the kids left the focus group, they were handed their cash honorarium and invited to take home a boom box of their choice from the display downstairs in the lobby.

Guess what color every single kid took home?

Black. They had just finished telling researchers, "whatever you do, don't make it black." What people say they'll do, buy and like can be very different from they actually do, buy and like.

Which is the problem with hypothetical research questions. "Would you like it better if it we did this?" "Would you buy it if we bundled it with that?"

I don't know about you, but the way I spend my hypothetical time and my hypothetical money is a lot different than the way I spend my real time and money. But people want to look good, sound intelligent, and be helpful. They tend to give the answers that sound good and make them look good.

They also tend to be negative and critical. Which is why, when you're doing your market research in whatever form you do it, don't ask what people think. Don't ask, "What do you think of this?"

Because something happens in the translation between your mouth and their ears. You asked, "What do you think of XYZ?" but they heard, "What's wrong with XYZ?" So that's what they tell you. You've unwittingly triggered their critic reflex, and they will go on and on about the bad stuff. They will actually look for and find things to change and correct, because they think that's what you asked them.

The Fix: Go undercover.

Here comes a non-scientific paraphrase of a famous physics guy named Heisenberg. He even has a principle named after him, and it says that the very act of research and observation can change the outcome of the study. And he was talking about atoms and molecules in the physical world. If the act of observation can change how stuff we can't see behaves, imagine how much it can change stuff we can see. Like people.

When people know they're part of a research study, they aren't themselves. They're research participants. They're on their toes, thinking twice, trying to "get it right," making sure they don't look dumb or duped.

I was shopping in the electronics section of a store, bought the latest whiz bang gizmo that would organize my life, and when I was less than 15 feet away from the counter, a woman armed with a clipboard approached me. Research!

She wanted to know how I rated the product knowledge and customer service of the electronics staff, relative to the purchase I had just made. (Her words, not mine. Hear how researchers talk?)

The guy that served me was still standing behind the counter, within range of a "hey, howareya!" How likely was it for me to say the guy was as dumb as a post and rude to boot? Even if he was, how smart would that make me look for having bought something from such a twit?

So I told her the guy was knowledgeable and helpful. Which he had been. I told the truth. Of course it was true. Because the guy knew from the moment he clocked in that morning that there would be a lady with a clipboard asking every single customer to rate his performance. He knew he was being observed, and I'm sure he kicked his internal Mr. Wizard and Service-With-A-Smile modules up a notch for the day.

I've seen respondents say they've heard of a company that I made up and that it had a good reputation for quality products, too. Because they wanted to appear well-informed.

I've heard people say they were patients at a hospital that didn't exist. They just liked being asked and wanted to answer more questions about a topic that was important to them.

So if you want the real answers, the real reasons people do, say or want something, you have to do your research when people don't know they're part of a research study. Or, in the case of Sony, when they think the research study is over.

Here are a couple of examples to spark some ideas.

Hang out with the target audience.

Do you want to know what low income, inner city, elderly men think or need? Volunteer at a community center. Play some chess, bridge or backgammon. That's what the marketing director for a non-profit social services agency did.

But chat, don't interrogate. See what comes up, what's important, what makes them smile and what makes them rant. Sometimes you get the best research when you don't know what it is you want to know. But you always know it when you hear it.

Acme Hospital wanted me to help them find out whether it had a chance of attracting pregnant women who lived 30 miles away to have their babies at Acme. The competition was Hometown Hospital, which was only a few minutes away.

Acme wanted to find out what the local women thought of Hometown Hospital and what (if any-thing) it would take to get them to make the drive to Acme Hospital.

Forget the focus groups. For a mom-to-be to say that she would drive 30 miles to have her baby might sound reckless, and it would be difficult to get the real answers if the women were worried about preserving and presenting a good mom-to-be image.

So I put on some loose clothing and spent the day pushing a shopping cart around the local Toys 'R' Us in the Hometown area.

When I saw a pregnant woman, or a woman who already had a young child, I approached her and said, "Excuse me, I know this is rather personal, but I couldn't help noticing that you have a young one, and I just found out I'm pregnant. My husband and I are moving here soon, and I was wondering . . . where's the best place to have a baby?"

Not "where's the best place around here?" or "is Hometown Hospital where you had your baby?" or "have you heard of Acme Hospital?" Just "where's the best place" to have a baby.

The answers were beyond interesting. They were insightful. No one said that Hometown Hospital was the best place. They said it was the only place. Turns out that the vast majority of women felt "stuck" with Hometown; there wasn't much of a fan club for the local facility.

Then there was the group of women who answered the "where's the best place" question with, "Definitely NOT Hometown Hospital." These women encouraged me to leave town to have my baby, and they suggested two other hospitals—neither of which was Acme Hospital.

So Acme learned that there were essentially two audiences in this outlying market: women who won't leave town to have a baby and women who will. They also identified competitors they hadn't even considered before. Hometown Hospital was not a competitor at all; the other two out-of-town hospitals were.

They also learned that for women who were willing to leave town, Acme Hospital barely registered on the radar screen, so their marketing budget had better include advertising and direct mail strategies to increase awareness and visibility.

I learned that when you do undercover research in Toys 'R' Us, leave your wallet home. I dropped a hundred bucks on pool toys for my family.

Observe, listen and lurk

Community Bank told me not to worry about Behemoth Bank, their competitor. "Nobody likes them," the marketing director said, because Behemoth was impersonal and treated people like an account number. Community Bank, on the other hand, was the local, friendly, customer-focused bank.

I visited a couple of Behemoth Bank branches anyway. I dressed in business attire so that any self-respecting banker would consider me a "live one" for potential deposits. I entered the lobby of the first branch, checked my watch, and went to a brochure rack.

Within 60 seconds, an employee walked over, pointed out the free coffee and invited me to help myself while I browsed. If I had any questions, she'd be glad to answer them, she said. Her name was Maggie. I also met Liz, Ralph and Christine when I visited their respective branches later in the day.

Then I visited a Community Bank branch (where they didn't know me). I went to the brochure rack and checked my watch. After I'd read four, tri-fold brochures, I walked around. There was no one at the New Accounts desk. There was no one in line for a teller, or Retail Banker, as they liked to call themselves at the friendly Community Bank.

No one approached me or even made eye contact. Maybe they thought I was casing the joint. Maybe they had called the FBI and were waiting for someone to haul me away. Finally, I was tired of waiting, so I asked someone where the rest room was. She asked me if I were a customer.

"Not likely," I wanted to say.

I went back to the marketing director at Community Bank and told him he was right. Community Bank did not have to worry about Behemoth Bank. They had to worry about themselves first.

Now what?

Get out of the office. Put down the data and the information and go look around. Research can give you all kinds of data. From data you will likely gather some information. But information isn't what you're after. You want insight from your research, something the competition has likely missed. From insight comes inspiration. That's what research should do for you.

I'll bet your best and favorite family photos are candid shots. Captured when the subject didn't know you had a lens aimed at them. The same thing goes for your customers and capturing their real thoughts and dreams. Dig deep. Look for the real answers, when people don't know you're looking.

Mistake #5

We all look alike.

No matter what business you're in, you probably walk and talk a lot like the other people who do what you do. Your target audience thinks your products and services, probably your marketing, too, are pretty much the same as everyone else's in that category.

A bank's a bank. Dry cleaning is dry cleaning. Consultants are a dime a dozen. Everyone knows a financial planner, and who isn't related to at least one real estate agent, if not by blood, then by marriage?

A lot of people I work with pound their fists and righteously proclaim how different, better, faster, experienced, specialized and/or affordable their products and services are. They think that quality, service and value sets their business apart.

A lot of them also think the Statue of Liberty is in New York.

Wrong on both counts. Quality, service and value get you in the game; they don't make you unique. And the Statue of Liberty is technically located in New Jersey.

But here's the good news. The more two things are alike, the more important every tiny difference becomes, and the more impact every difference has in setting you apart—because your prospects are looking for the differences.

Think about identical twins. What's the first thing you do when you encounter a pair of identically dressed identical twins? You try to find a way to tell them apart, right. You're looking closely, trying to find that tiny distinguishing mark or feature that is different.

My neighbor has identical twin boys. Apparently they are a rare kind of identical twins, because they are more identical than your run-of-the-mill identical twins. (Or so the mom tells me.)

"Which one is this?" I asked her when I was visiting the newborns.

She glanced at the baby I was pointing to in the crib and said, "That's Jared."

"How can you tell?" I asked. They looked like graduates of a secret cloning experiment to me.

"It's easy," she said. "Jared has a tiny little wrinkle on his left ear. Riley doesn't."

"That's it?" I looked at the twin on the left, the twin on the right. I studied their ears. Sure enough, the twin on the right had a wrinkle on his left ear. (To be honest, if I were their mom, I don't think I would have cut those little hospital bracelets off quite as soon.)

Yet I had to admit it. That one, tiny wrinkle made a difference. All the difference in the world, actually, because it set the boys apart. And the same is true for your business. Even a small difference can have a big impact on setting you apart. Again, because they are looking for it!

The Fix (Part 1):
Find your points of difference

How do you find your points of difference? Start with all your points of contact, anywhere you come in contact with a customer or prospect.

Voice mail greeting	Email signature
Front door	How you answer phones
Business card	Proposal cover sheet
Parking lot entrance	Invoice
Reception area	Ads, brochures, flyers
Home page	You get the idea...

Look at what you're doing for each of your touch points, and then find out what the competition is doing for each of theirs. If you have several competitors, you might need several lists. If you want to make it easier, just consider what most businesses in your category do for each touch point. (As in, what do most bankers, dry cleaners, consultants or name-your-category do?)

Look it all over, and find the areas where you and the competition look alike, where you're essentially doing the same thing, or where you're doing the expected, usual or ordinary thing.

The obvious question is, "How can you do it differently?" And remember, you're looking for a wrinkle, not plastic surgery.

I know a good place to start making changes. Your voice mail greeting. When I speak to business audiences, I usually ask if there's anyone in the room who does NOT know how to leave a voicemail. Everyone knows how, so no one ever raises a hand on that question.

Why then, I ask, do nine out of 10 business voicemail greetings provide instructions on to how to leave a voicemail? "At the sound of the beep, please leave me a message, and I'll return your call as soon as possible."

Voicemail greetings all sound alike. No one listens to or cares aboutyour greeting because they know what you're going to say—the same thing everybody says. So take advantage of a free, easy, fast way to stand out in a big way. Change your voice mail greeting. Mark this page, and do it now, even.

In the world of professional speaking, speakers throw around something called a 1-sheet. It's a combination flyer, ad, brochure, direct mail piece. Essentially, it's a marketing communications tool we use to get on a meeting planner's radar screen. (Some speakers think a 1-sheet will sell their services and land them a booking, but you've read Mistake #2 and know better.)

Meeting planners get PDFs and piles of 1-sheets every day. The bulk of them are 8-1/2 x 11 vertical flyers with a giant photo of the speaker, and either the speaker's name or her topic is printed large enough to be read from across the Interstate.

My 1-sheet is horizontal, and my photo is the size of a postage stamp. And because I know meeting planners don't care about me (they care about themselves), my headline is about them, not me or my topic. They are just a few tiny differences that might at least cause the meeting planner to pause before she decides where to pile or file my 1-sheet.

Is my calendar booked solid? Not yet. Do the meeting planners remember my 1-sheet when I call to follow-up? Most do. (Naming my company Blah, Blah, Blah, instead of Langhans Something Or Other, hasn't hurt, either.)

As you ponder points of difference, ask yourself what you could do if you weren't a [blank]. What could you do if you weren't a bank, or a hospital or an accountant? The goal is to stand out for your category, so perhaps you will find inspiration in someone else's industry. The first hospital to offer valet parking wasn't thinking like a hospital. They were thinking like a hotel.

The Fix (Part 2):
The single most effective way to stand out

Remember the twins? When they get older, even if they continue to look like clones, there's still one, sure-fire way people will be able to tell them apart. Maybe not on sight, but certainly after they get to know the boys a bit.

Personality. The brothers will have unique per-sonalities. In fact, what do you think those twins will do on April Fool's Day in the fifth grade? Switch places, right? They'll try to fake out their friends and teachers, and they'll probably get away with it for, oh, about an hour or two.

Because you can't fake someone else's personal-ity. And that's what makes "personality" the most effective way your company can distinguish itself from the competition. Your competition can't copy your unique personality.

Here's my favorite example. There can't be many businesses that are more alike than stock brokerage firms. I can buy the same stock or mutual fund from any of them and pay the same price. Three of them still stand out in my mind.

There was what used to be called Smith Barney. John Houseman spoke directly into the camera with his British accent and the message was, "At Smith Barney, we make money the old fashioned way. We earrrrrnnn it."

E.F. Hutton's commercial featured a busy restaurant scene with every table occupied by diners engaged in scintillating conversations. The camera zoomed in on one table, and we picked up just a snippet of conversation:

". . . my broker is E.F. Hutton, and E.F. Hutton says . . . ."

Silence. The entire restaurant freezes and leans over to hear what E.F. Hutton had to say.

And then there was Merrill Lynch. The bull in the china shop commercial. Literally, they had a full-grown bull with horns walk through the aisles of a china shop. I don't remember a word that was said, or if a word was even said, because I was mesmerized by the action, by the perfectly calm way that bull navigated his way back out the front door without causing a single tea cup to quiver in its saucer.

Three different firms that each used their marketing to establish three different personalities. A conservative, upper crust personality for Smith Barney. A consultative advisor for E.F. Hutton. And an aggressive, yet precise and strategic persona for Merrill Lynch. The beauty is that each personality attracted a different kind of investor, as well.

Now, don't worry. You don't have to buy television ads to establish a personality. Any business can have one, but not every one does.

Come to my party.

How do you find or create a personality for your business, product or service? You describe your company as if it were a person.

Easy, some people say. "My company is conservative, professional, customer-focused and dedicated to providing shareholder value."

That's not a person. That's a sentence right out of an annual report. Let me make it easier.

Pretend I've invited you to a party at my house. You ask if you can bring a friend, someone I don't know. The "friend" you're bringing is your business. As any hostess would, I ask you to tell me about your friend.

Would you say, "I'm bringing a conservative, professional, customer-focused person who's dedicated to shareholder value"?

Of course not. You'd say, "Wait till you meet Bill. He's a friendly guy who makes new friends every where he goes." Or, "I'm bringing Sue. She just moved here, and I think she's a little homesick."

Tell me more. Picture your business as a person at the party. How will he or she behave? Is your friend/business going to mingle, or will we have to draw your friend/business into conversation? Does your friend/business have a sense of humor? Are there topics we better not bring up at the party? Is your friend/business good looking or cute? Memorable or forgettable? Will your friend/business help me clean up?

After you have a visual picture of your company as a walking, talking party-goer, ask your friend/business to write me a thank you note for including him/her in the party. What did your friend/business like the most? Whom did s/he meet that was memorable? The idea here is to find your company's "voice," and then use it.

Just because your company or product is the best, or the leader, that doesn't mean she will talk that way at the party. Just because she's a leader doesn't mean, at the party, that she'll boss people around and tout her credentials and experience every chance she gets.

But isn't that what a lot of marketing sounds like? Find your personality, your voice. Then use it. Because the best marketing sounds like a letter from a good friend, not an annual report or resume. The best marketing is feels like a dialogue, not a monologue.

Now what?

Make your list of touch points, look at the competition, look at other industries. Go to a party, but don't wear your marketing hat. See if you can meet a new friend. . .your business.

Mistake #6

We are fooled by facts, but love logic anyway.

If your marketing appeals to reason, it may have no appeal at all.

Take milk, for example. Before the wildly successful "Got Milk?" campaign, milk consumption was in a steady downward spiral for 13 years. Remember the "Milk does a body good" and "Every*body* needs milk" commercials? They were informative ads that reminded an allegedly health-conscious world how healthy milk was. If more people knew it was good for them, they'd drink more of it. Sounds logical.

But nobody was buying it. Literally or figuratively. Milk was not, and is not, a health food. People didn't drink it because it was good for them, and they weren't going to drink more of it just because the ads listed all the nutrients and showed healthy, happy people drinking it.

You drink milk because you can't eat a gooey, chewy chocolate chip cookie without it. You just can't. The "Got Milk!" campaign captured what was really important to people about drinking milk. It connected to why people like milk, instead of trying to convince them they should drink milk. The campaign made you thirsty, not smart.

And it worked. In the first year the campaign ran, milk consumption increased 2 percent. That's 100 million more dollars worth of milk. (I've always wondered if chocolate chip cookie consumption made a parallel ascent, as well.)

An isolated case, you say? OK, here are some facts that should, but won't, change your buying behavior. Just the facts, no hocus pocus advertising voodoo.

We're talking about orange juice, this time. Let's say you want to buy the ripest, tastiest, juiciest oranges you can find to make fresh-squeezed orange juice.

How do you buy oranges? How do you judge quality? How will you know a ripe, tasty, juicy orange when you see one?

"They're orange, Terri. Deep, dark orange." That's how most people answer my question.

Wrong. On the day they're picked from the tree, oranges are as ripe, tasty and juicy as they'll ever be. And when they're picked, they might not be orange at all. Some might be greenish, yellowish or any combination of citrus colors.

They show up orange in your grocery store only because on the way there, they make a little pit stop. They stop to be sprayed with a chemical that I can't pronounce, let alone spell. The chemical reaction on the skin of the orange is what turns an orange orangier.

So there, then. I know this, not because I'm a native Orange County, California resident (which I am), but because Harry Beckwith, author of *Selling the Invisible*, told me so. I've since informed my audiences, and when I do, there's always someone there that knows a farmer, was a farmer, or professionally picked an orange once and tells me it's true.

"The same is true for bananas!" a guy once shouted from the back of the room. "Except that bananas turn yellow, " he added. (I hate it when the audience steals my punch line.)

That being said, now that you know, as I do, that color has nothing to do with how ripe, tasty or juicy an orange is, are you going to change the way you buy them?

Didn't think so. Me either.

Don't get me wrong. Facts and logic are important, but they are by no means a secret weapon for you, or your competition, to wield. After all, what do you do if it looks like the competition has all the facts in their favor? What if they have bigger marketing budgets, more store locations, better prices, a broader scope of services, more experience? Do you cringe at the thought of a logical comparison or side-by-side demonstration? Do you just throw in the towel?

Take heart, and put down the towel.

The Fix: Emotions are more powerful than facts.

Consider, instead, the comparison of my American Express card and my Visa card. My American Express card costs me $75 a year. My Visa card is free.

My American Express is a charge card; I have to pay the entire balance every month, or else suffer the humiliation and shame of a rejected card. My Visa is a credit card; I have the flexibility of making payments or paying the balance.

I cant' use my American Express card everywhere. It's accepted in fewer places than Visa.

So let's look at this logically. My American Express card costs more, is accepted in fewer places and is less flexible. My Visa card is free, flexible when it comes to payments and it is "everywhere I want to be." Which card makes more sense?

Duh. Visa.

Do you have an American Express card? 'Fess up. More than 25 million people do.

Are they nuts? Are you nuts?

Didn't I just prove that Visa is the logical, sensible card to carry? It makes no sense to carry American Express. Then why do we?

How about "membership has its privileges"? I know, I know. I, too, can come up with all kinds of rational reasons that sound good to justify carrying my American Express card.

That's precisely why facts are, indeed, important. And why emotions are more powerful. Emotions drive the decision. We use the facts and logic to justify it. The real reason we do something is usually emotional. The "reason that sounds good" is almost always factual or logical.

Your prospects and customers need both. Facts and feelings. When you build your business and your marketing around both, people will do things that make no sense whatsoever.

Like paying a couple bucks for and iced tea that I know I could make myself at home for pennies. Yet every day, I use precious fossil fuel to transport myself three miles down the road to Starbucks. I know there's a good chance I'll have to stand in line, but I go anyway. I know I may or may not be able to resist buying a box of chocolate covered cherries while I stand in line. But I go anyway. If I don't resist the cherries, I console myself with the fact that cherries are fruit, and you need five servings of fruit or vegetables a day, right? (Sounds good to me.)

And if all that's not illogical enough for you, the real clincher is that Starbucks is known for coffee. Not tea. Not cherries. And I go anyway.

Starbucks sells coffee; that's a famous fact. And at one point in their history, even their CEO thought they were all about coffee. The best coffee, from the highest-quality beans, ground a certain way, brewed with filtered water, at the right temperature, to perfection.

But then the CEO heard one of the employees share this insight:

"Starbucks is not in the coffee business serving people," he said. "We are in the people business serving coffee."

Touché.

Starbucks is not about engineering a great cup of coffee or tea, although the facts could certainly prove they do. Starbucks is about providing an emotional experience. Providing a place in which I feel welcome, around people who make me feel important. A place where, even if I didn't spend two bucks a day on iced tea, they'd still let me use their electricity. And write my book.

Now what?

Emotion is the vehicle that gets you inside someone's wall. Facts are the passengers that get to jump out, once you're inside. It's easy and tempting to come up with a list of reasons your product or service is the best choice. There are so many important things the prospect needs to know in order to come to the correct, logical decision.

But facts are cold, impersonal and preachy. Resist them like the plague. Same goes for clichés.

Instead, ask yourself, and the marketing decision makers you work with, these questions:

1. What is the single most important thing you want people to know, think or believe about your product, service or company? Focus your message on that one thing.

2. When it's all said and done, what do you want them to feel? Focus everything you say, everything you do, and everything you don't do, on that. Your marketing should not show an emotion. It should make people feel one.

Mistake #7

We don't go far enough.

Bear with me. We need a flashback scene.

Remember how I said, way back in Mistake #1, that people would line up outside my door wanting me to "do" some marketing for them? And remember how I said marketing isn't something you "do," that it involves a whole lot more than just marketing communications?

Well, after a while, people knew better than to come to my door and say they needed to "do" some marketing. That's because they got tired of hearing me say "help or hinder" and hearing me ask all those butt-insky questions about other things they could do to reach their goal besides doing marketing communications.

So instead, people eventually came to my door and said, "Quick, Terri, how would you market this?"

And the scary thing is, I had an answer for them.

No, it's not a checklist or a patent-pending, proprietary model with a clever acronym that stands for M.A.R.K.E.T or S.U.C.C.E.S.S. Essentially, it's a thought-process-without-a-name.

Yet unfortunately, a big mistake often happens half-way through the thought process. It did back then, and it still does. Essentially, people ignore the second half—they don't go far enough with their planning and implementation. And it happens regardless of whether it's my process, one of their own, or a patent-pending one with initials.

So here's Terri's-thought-process-without-a-name. I'll walk you through it, step by step, and at the half-way point, you'll run into Mistake #7. And then I'll show you how to fix it.

Once you know "where you are" and "where you want to be," and you know what's helping and hindering the sale and use of the product or service here are the words that click through my brain to spark the important marketing decisions:

Attract

Communicate

Respond

Involve

Manage

Track

Attract: Who are you trying to attract and what will attract them to your product or service?

"Who," of course, means your "target audience." Acknowledging who they are in a descriptive, demographic sense isn't enough. You need to truly understand them and what's important to them. If you don't know what makes them sit bolt upright in bed at 2 o'clock in the morning, or what they think of you and your competition, then it's time to go undercover and find out.

"What will attract them?" refers to your attraction factors. What is it that will stand out and attract attention? What is important, personally, to your audience? Remember, connect before you convince. Perhaps your points of difference, and your personality will come into play here, too.

Communicate: How are you going to communicate your message, and what will that message be? We would be talking about a media plan here, if paid advertising were one of your marketing activities. But we're also talking about all the other ways you can choose to deliver your message.

I used to call this step in my thought process a MAP, as in Marketing Action Plan. But now, given how I poked fun at acronyms a few pages ago, I'll just gloss right over those capital letters and let you decide for yourself whether you want to remember them that way or not.

Regardless of what you call it, you do have to have a marketing action plan. You need to decide which marketing activities you're going to use to reach your target audience, get on their radar screen and attract their interest. (Notice how I didn't say, "sell"?)

Be careful! Give it serious thought. Too many people like to invoke what I call the Bad RAM shortcut method of deciding their action plan. RAM on your computer stands for Random Access Memory, and it is a valuable shortcut for finding and retrieving information on your hard drive. That's good RAM.

Bad RAM stands for Random Acts of Marketing. You know you're in trouble when you hear yourself or others saying, "Let's try X." Let's try radio, or an open house, pod casting, networking, whatever.

Here's another brain dump of activities and actions to consider:

Advertising
- •TV, radio
- • Newspaper
- • Magazine/trades
- • Outdoor
- • Giveaways/trinkets

PR/Publicity
Direct Mail

Email
Networking
Trade show
Speaking/seminars
Web/Internet
Telemarketing
Referral strategy

When you consider the activities that will become your marketing action plan, think *monthly*. What combination of activities are you going to do each month? People tend to think about marketing in a "let's try this next" mind set, instead of looking at it as a mix and part of a plan. Set your course for at least 90 days at a time.

Be sure and consider activities on a personal or individual level. What are you, personally, (or someone who works with or for you) going to do every month to communicate your message?

I think it helps to literally circle the listed activities that you plan to use on a monthly basis, and then do them for the next three months. It may not be a marketing plan that becomes a two-inch thick, spiral-bound tome that doubles as a door-stop, but it's written down, and you can keep track of it simply.

So, if your plan is Networking, Referrals and Direct Mail, then how many networking meetings will you (or someone representing your company) attend every month? Every week? For your Referral strategy, how will you stay in touch—every 30 days for the next 90 days—with the people who can send you more business?

If you're using direct mail, you need the right list and an outstanding creative design and concept. The minute you put direct mail in your marketing mix, your competition is no longer the other folks who do what you do. Your competition is every marketer out there with a postage meter. Your message must stand out and be credible, but it doesn't have to cost a lot. Most of what's in the mail will be that blatant, boastful blah, blah, blah stuff. Go for concept and connection over color and noise.

Direct mail also works best when there's an offer attached. "Remember me when you need me" is a valid use of direct mail, but if you're using it as a response strategy, and not one to build awareness, then you need an offer.

"Hire me" is not an offer. "Call or visit my web site for a free article on direct mail success factors" is an offer.

For me, and for many others who run a service business, direct mail works best when followed up with a phone call. Which would mean putting a circle around Telemarketing on the list. (But don't flinch. You're not cold calling during dinner.) Set your monthly plan to include a weekly number of follow-up calls to the direct mail prospects whom you think have the greatest potential fit for your product or service.

Respond: I'm not talking about how your prospects will respond, as in whether they'll call or click or come into the store. I'm talking about how YOU will respond. When that person raises a symbolic hand and expresses an interest, having seen or heard your communication from the above activities, how will YOU respond? What is it that you want to put in that outstretched hand?

Your product? A contract? A sale? You know better than that! But actually, it's OK this time, for this reason. You're in strategy mode. This is precisely the point in the thought process to remind yourself of where you want to be, remind yourself of your ultimate goal. For me, it might be a booking for a speech or workshop participants. For you it might be sales, clients, customers or new projects.

Now's the time to do a reality check and ask yourself whether the mix you've circled in your action plan is going to lead you to your ultimate, No. 1 goal. Let's assume it will.

Because that's when big Mistake #7 happens. Right here at the "Respond" step.

Everybody stops. Literally, that's the mistake. Everybody stops thinking and doing, once they've thought through Attract, Communicate and Respond. It's as if they draw a line and think their marketing plan is finished. (Food is done. People are finished.)

No! We still have Involve, Manage and Track to talk about, the steps that are "below the line." But most people, deep down, despite having read Mistakes #1 through #6, want to be finished. They want to sit back and wait for the phone to ring or the emails to come. So they sit back and wait for thirsty horses to show up at the watering hole.

If you wait for response, you're going to be disappointed. Few people do what you want them to do, when you want them to do it, just because you asked them to do it. Most marketing, if it doesn't generate an inquiry or a question, boils down to "remember me when you need me." (This is especially true if you're marketing a service.)

The Fix: Go below the line.

You have to go below the line if you want your marketing to generate response and make you memorable. You have to have tactics and strategies to keep people involved with you until they are ready to do the No. 1 thing you want them to do.

Involve: How can you stay involved with prospects until they are ready to do the No. 1 thing you want them to do?

Let's see, if they responded to the email, or direct mail, and they didn't say "no," but they weren't ready for "yes" quite yet, what else can you do that will help them remember you when they need you? What can you do that will bring them closer to that ultimate "yes"?

Maybe you offer a free subscription to your electronic newsletter, or you send them a more detailed piece of information, a product demo, a free sample. Maybe you suggest one of those activities, but send them send a direct mail card once a quarter, too.

The point here is that you must have enough other ways to be visible and stay top-of-mind, without becoming a pest. You've got to keep prospects involved, before and after they do the No. 1 thing you wanted them to do.

I worked with a cardiologist once who mailed two different direct mail pieces to a target audience of senior citizens. The mailings let people know that they didn't have to live with leg pain, that if the pain was caused by a circulatory problem, and not arthritis, laser angioplasty might be a solution that would make them pain free.

The No. 1 goal was to generate angioplasty patients. Amazingly enough, five people immediately called and scheduled appointments with the doctor, and every one of them had the procedure. Boy was he happy.

The plan, though, included a couple of other "involvement" steps, because we knew this would be a major decision for the patient, and it would more than likely require discussion and research before the patient felt informed enough to schedule the procedure.

So one of the steps we built into the plan was a free screening at the doctor's office. Our undercover research told us that senior citizens just accepted leg pain as "part of getting older," which was a shame, because relief was relatively simple, if the pain was caused by poor circulation.

And the screening was even simpler. Measure the blood pressure in the arm, and then in the ankle. If they didn't match, the leg pain was a blood flow problem, not arthritic wear and tear. Laser angioplasty could fix it.

So the idea was, if patients called from the direct mail piece, the staff would tell them about the free screening. If they weren't quite ready for the screening, they could request an educational brochure about leg pain and the laser angioplasty procedure. The brochure, of course, mentioned the free screening, too.

A means to a greater end. The direct mail, the brochure and the screening were a means to a greater end, a means to achieve the No. 1 goal of attracting new patients.

In addition to the five people who called, came in for the screening and had their laser procedure, 98 more people requested a brochure so that they could learn more about the problem and the laser solution. That's 98 people who "raised their hands" and said, essentially, "I'm interested, tell me more."

It was a huge failure.

The doctor would not go below the line. He had 98 prospects with leg pain, and he didn't want to do any follow-up. He mailed the brochures, and that was the end. He could have sent 98 follow-up cards or letters. Made a few phone calls?

"I don't want to bother them," he said. He was happy with the business he got above-the-line.

I call that an advertising success and a marketing failure.

Manage: So, if you are not like the cardiologist, and you have a variety of communication tools and involvement steps you're willing take, you're going to need to manage them. You can't do it on human memory fuel.

I am bi-lingual (ambidextrous?) when it comes to using a Macintosh and a PC, and I'd be the first person to buy a digital toothbrush, if they ever come out with one. But I also use a good-old-fashioned tickler file to manage my marketing action plan and its involvement steps. (If your brain has already made a picture of what a good-old-fashioned tickler file is and how it works, go ahead, skip to the next bold face heading. You won't hurt my feelings.)

My tickler file is in a file drawer, with 43 folders in it. One for each of the 12 months and one for each of the 31 days that could be in a month.

Let's pretend it's June 4th and I've been making follow-up calls on some emails to meeting planners. I talk to a "live one." But her conference just ended and the last thing she wants to think about is planning the next one. But she did like chatting about my Maverick Marketing program, and agrees it might be a good fit. Just not now.

She didn't use those words, but I know that's the real story, so I ask, "can I gently stay on your radar screen now and then, without becoming a pest?"

She says yes. I tag her in my database as "radar screen" and schedule a "to do" follow-up call for September. Then I grab four direct mail postcards and address them to her. I put one in the file folder with a 31 on it, which means on June 31st I'll reach in and mail it. Along with anything else I find filed in that day's folder.

I put another card in the "July" folder, one in "August," and one in "September." On July 1st I'll see that post card and decide whether to mail it right then, or drop it one of the other "day" folders and mail it then.

The bottom line is, no matter what your system is, use one. Don't rely on your memory to manage the various involvement steps you build into your MAP. (There, I used the acronym. I give up.)

Track: The last step in Terri's-thought-process-that-doesn't-spell-anything is to decide what you're going to track and how you're going to do it. Flashback to Mistake #2 on measuring key indicators in addition to tracking your No. 1 goal.

Your involvement steps and communication tools are the key indicators I was talking about.

How many phone calls, email inquiries, web hits, requests for additional information, screenings, newsletter subscriptions did you have? Everything you decide to do above the line, and everything you do below the line should drive prospects right back toward the ultimate goal. So rather than waiting to see whether you hit your No. 1 goal, track the indicators along the way, too.

Almost always, when I work with someone who isn't consistently reaching the No. 1 goal, that someone is not consistently doing the work to generate the key indicators along the way. They only went to one networking meeting instead of four, made contact with a handful of referral sources instead of 20, and the direct mail cards went out, but the phone calls never did.

Now what?

Work the plan, and it will work. You might be spending money above the line, but you will make money below the line. Better yet, you'll also build relationships with your prospects and customers, and those are the best—and my favorite—kind of results.

The End

Put your
marketing hat back on.

It's safe. Your brain has been fortified, I hope, by these seven mistakes and seven fixes. And just so you don't focus on the mistake side of the fence—the stuff you're not supposed to do—here's a summary of the stuff I want you to do.

You'll stand out, get better results and win more business if you do.

#1

"Marketing" is more than communications and promotion. Expand your definition. What's going to help you get from where you are to where you want to be, and what's hindering your progress? Do more of the former, and fix what you can of the latter.

#2

Marketing communications and advertising don't sell anything to anyone. Have realistic expectations of what marketing communications can do. Like increase visibility and awareness, create an image or personality, and generate response in the form of curious callers and people who want to know more about what you do and what it can do for them.

#3

Connect before you convince. Find out what's important, personally, to your prospect. Stand out from all the hoopla, the blatant and boastful chest-pounding messages consumers avoid. Stand out by virtue of being customer-focused, in a way that gets them to peek over the wall, lower the draw-bridge and invite you inside their fortress.

#4

Go undercover. Go beyond data and information. Dig for insight, for the real answers. And don't settle for the answers that just sound good, or make the consumer look good. Observe, listen and lurk. Do so when they are being themselves, not subjects of a study.

#5

The more alike two things are, the more important every difference becomes. Create a few points of difference from looking at your points of contact. Resist the usual, the expected and the ordinary in everything you do. And remember that the single most important way you can set your business apart is the same way people are set apart: personality. It's free, it's easy and no one can copy yours.

Milk and orange juice, American Express and Visa—emotions are more powerful than facts. Emotion is the vehicle that gets you inside the hearts and minds of your customers. Facts are the passengers they'll use to justify their decision. Use both. Create an experience that defies logic. If Starbucks can do it for a glass of iced tea, surely you can, too.

Attract

Communicate

Respond

Involve

Manage

Track

Go below the line. That's where real results, loyal relationships and success are built.

If you want to market like every one else out there, you certainly don't need my help.

If you truly want to stand out and be different, here a few great ways we might work together.

I speak to business audiences who want to stand out, get better results from their marketing and sell more products and services. I can do any or all of the 7 Mistakes in formats that range from a 45-minute keynote to a 3-day workshop and road show.

My Maverick Marketing 1-Day Workshop is typically held three or four times a year, and I also work 1:1 with a handful of companies or business owners who want better results from their marketing, but *don't* want to spend a boatload of money hiring an in-house guru or big outside consulting firm.

Whether it's the public workshop or working together 1:1 by phone or face-to-face, I typically zero in on four key marketing areas:

1. How to distinguish yourself and your message in the marketplace and from the competition.

2. Finding, attracting and influencing the choice of your target audience.

3 Deciding the right mix of marketing activities and tactics that will generate response and referrals, as well as the message that will be memorable and meaningful.

4. Benchmarks for measuring success and tracking results.

Call or click if you'd like to explore these or other bright ideas that will make your marketing less ordinary and more effective.

(800) 207-0015

Speaking:
www.BlahBlahBlah.us

1:1 and Marketing Workshop:
www.MaverickMarketing.com

Blahg:
www.AnythingButBlah.com

The 7 Marketing Mistakes Book, CD, DVDs:
www.The7MarketingMistakes.com